Bridges of Hope

The CAFOD/DLT Lent Book 2001

David Adam ✦ Margaret Atkins
Imelda Davidson ✦ Margaret Hebblethwaite
Charles Hedley ✦ Kate McFarlane

Bridges of Hope

Reflections on the
Scripture Readings for Lent 2001

IT'S TIME FOR JUSTICE
CAFOD

DARTON·LONGMAN+TODD

First published in Great Britain in 2000 by

CAFOD
Romero Close
Stockwell Road
London SW9 9TY

Darton, Longman and Todd Ltd
Spencer Court
140-142 Wandsworth High Street
London SW18 4JJ

ISBN 0 232 52392 4

Cover photo: Jon Spaull
Design: Garry Lambert

Printed and bound in Great Britain by Page Bros, Norwich, Norfolk

Contents

About the authors

David Adam is vicar of Holy Island, Northumberland, and author of many best-selling books, including *Forward to Freedom*.

Margaret Atkins lectures in theology at Trinity and All Saints University College, Leeds.

Imelda Davidson works in the parliamentary liaison office of the South African Catholic Bishops' Conference.

Margaret Hebblethwaite is a writer and journalist. She lives in the village of Santa María in Misiones in Paraguay.

Charles Hedley is rector of St James's church, Piccadilly, London.

Kate McFarlane is the Justice and Peace fieldworker for the Brentwood Diocese.

Introduction

As always the writers in the CAFOD Lent reflections chip away at the surface of the lectionary readings and reveal a God who defies our expectations. A God we meet in silent prayer and in boisterous advocacy for justice; a God who accepts us as we are and who shows us how we can be something very different; a God who challenges and disturbs us and who wants us to find joy and happiness; a God of constant change and renewal and a God who remains still and unmoving in the midst of decay and disintegration.

What does it mean to live the gospel in a world that seems so unlike that of Jesus' first followers? What is astonishing is not the difference between what we are called to do but how doing what Jesus wants us to do remains so simple, and so unchanged. We are asked to love God with all our heart and with all our soul and with all our mind; and we are asked to love our neighbour as ourself. It is breathtakingly simple – and almost impossibly difficult.

The South African writer Imelda Davidson reminds us, 'In today's global village we are faced with the same question: "Who is my neighbour?" ' Christians believe that every human being is created in the image of God. We are all members of the same human family, deserving of the same dignity and respect, whatever our nationality or religion. People and money and information move around the world so quickly and easily today that the image of the single human family is becoming increasingly vivid and real. As in every family, our greed or our thoughtfulness is intimately linked to the misery or the fulfilment of our brothers and sisters.

In our increasingly globalised world it's impossible to pretend that there is no connection between our relatively secure and prosperous lives in Britain and the desperately impoverished and uncertain circumstances faced by more than one billion people in the world's poorest communities.

David Adam points out, 'When we ignore or abuse any part of God's creation we ignore or abuse our God. We are all part of the body of Christ. We cannot say that what we do in private does not hurt anybody for what we do influences our whole lives and the lives of those around us.' Charles Hedley shares this striking quotation with us: 'The issue is not, what will we give to the poor? It is, when will we stop taking from the poor?'

This is the mysterious and inexhaustible God revealed in *Bridges of Hope*. A God who hungers and thirsts for justice, who wants to use us to tilt the whole of creation in the direction of gospel values, yet who cares about the slightest bruise on a single child's heart; a God who seems to demand that we let go of every safety net and fall-back position, and who yet brings a peace and security beyond understanding.

Brendan Walsh

Imelda Davidson
Ash Wednesday to Saturday after Ash Wednesday

Ash Wednesday

Come back to me with all your heart

Jl 2:12-18; Ps 50:3-6, 12-14, 17; 2 Cor 5:20-6:2; Mt 6:1-6, 16-18

'Come back to Yahweh your God, for he is gracious and compassionate, slow to anger, rich in faithful love.'

(Joel 2: 13)

Ash Wednesday marks the beginning of Lent as a time of spiritual cleansing and renewal. It is a time for opening our hearts to God's transforming power. We are marked by ash as a sign of our commitment to this process of renewal and transformation. The readings today also point to an important aspect of Lent: we experience this season of the Church's journey both as community and as individuals.

The reading from Joel resonates strongly with memories of growing up as a Catholic on the Cape Flats of Cape Town – an area designated exclusively for 'Coloureds' under the apartheid regime in South Africa. Lent was the time when, as community, we responded to God's call to turn away from all that separated us from each other and from God. Ash Wednesday was welcomed as a second chance, a time to start afresh. And so it was that on Ash Wednesday we would stream to the various Christian churches on the Cape Flats to come as community before God to acknowledge our sins. And the God from whom we begged forgiveness is indeed a God who is all tenderness and compassion. For this was the God who had suffered with us through times of physical, emotional and political oppression.

Today, still, we know this God as the one who cries with us over children lost and found, over families broken and reconciled: the God who has always provided. It is the same God who has led us to freedom, and yet who continues to suffer with those whose lives remain unchanged, for in spite of the end of apartheid very many still experience poverty and strife.

Once again, on this Ash Wednesday, we come before God to ask forgiveness for the many ways in which we have failed to love. We come with heavy hearts; and with outstretched hands. Yet we also come before God deeply confident that our prayers will be heard. We come with absolute confidence that if we are truly repentant we will again be enfolded in the embrace of love and forgiveness that encompasses all.

This requires genuine commitment on our part to follow anew the path of the gospel. And so we embark on our Lenten journey mindful of Matthew's reminder that our Lenten practices of almsgiving, prayer and fasting are to be carried out with good hearts and pure intentions.

Thought for the day

What is my commitment as I begin my Lenten journey today? What are the things that keep me from fully loving God and others?

Prayer

Lord,
help me to experience these forty days of Lent
as a time to draw closer to you
and discern afresh your will for my life.
May I be always open to your Spirit moving within me.
Amen.

Thursday after Ash Wednesday

Choose life!

Dt 30:15-20; Ps 1; Lk 9:22-25

'If anyone wants to be a follower of mine, let him renounce himself and take up his cross every day and follow me.'

(Luke 9: 23)

We often see Lent in negative terms. We speak of what we are 'giving up' for Lent, of the 'sacrifices' we are making, of what we are denying ourselves. Yet Lent is a very positive time. A time for reviewing attitudes, habits and practices that have a destructive impact on our lives. A time for identifying our failings and finding ways to transform them into positive and life-giving forces.

Both the reading from Deuteronomy and the Psalm spell out very clearly that we have a fundamental choice to make. We can either choose God and God's ways, and receive life and ongoing nurturing from God; or we can choose life apart from God, a life that leads to isolation and destruction.

This is not a once-and-for-all choice. Every day, in each decision we make, large or small, we make a choice for life or against life. This can be seen in very practical ways, for example, in choosing to hold on to more than we need when there are so many people around us who have less than they need. We also make choices for or against life in the way in which we relate to people. When we use words that hurt or wound we are causing 'little deaths'.

The snide remarks we dismiss as insignificant might be remembered for a lifetime by those at whom they are targeted. And at a global level, decisions made by one country increasingly affect the lives of millions of people in another. In Africa, we often watch in horror as the fate of our nations, our children and our future generations are held to ransom by a few powerful and wealthy people living on the other side of the world.

Making choices that are life-giving is not always easy. It often comes at a price. Yet Jesus reminds us in the gospel reading that if you want to be his follower you have to take up your cross every day. Jesus did not promise an easy discipleship, but he did promise that he would be with us every step of the way.

Thought for the day

Are the daily choices that I make life-giving or destructive? How can I transform the negative choices into ones that have a positive impact on my life and the lives of others?

Prayer

Lord,
help me to remain rooted in your life-giving ways.
May the choices that I make today be shaped by your values of justice and freedom.
Grant that those whose lives I touch today may experience, through me, your love and peace.
Amen.

Friday after Ash Wednesday

The fast that pleases

Is 58:1-9; Ps 51:3-6, 18-19; Mt 9:14-15

'Is not this the sort of fast that pleases me:
to break unjust fetters,
to undo the thongs of the yoke,
to let the oppressed go free, and to break all yokes?'

(Isaiah 58: 6)

This reading from Isaiah was often used at special Masses in the days of the liberation struggle in South Africa. It spoke so clearly to our situation and confirmed that, whatever happened, our struggle was a just one. We had God on our side.

Much has changed since those days, yet these words from Isaiah continue to be as pertinent today as they were then. Even in our post-apartheid South Africa, with its wonderful constitution entrenching the freedom and dignity of every citizen, we are challenged to reflect anew on the kind of fast we offer to God. How do we come before God with a pleasing offering when so much poverty, injustice, violence, abuse and discrimination flourish in our land?

Perhaps we need to take a new look at the kind of fasting that the Church invites us to undertake during Lent. It is a fasting that begins with an external action, and leads us to an inner contemplation of the act of fasting itself, and its consequences. Fasting is a way of emptying ourselves of our self-centred desires and appetites so that we can be open to hearing the voices of those in need. Jesus fasted whilst in the desert in order to be open to hearing the cries of humanity – of all people everywhere – so that he could, when the time demanded it, respond to our need for salvation. The act that is pleasing to God is not fasting to the point of starvation or exhaustion for its own sake, but a fast that changes us, that opens us up to an awareness of God's will, that results in positive changes in people's lives.

When we let go of our own wants and desires and become focused on God working through us to respond to those in need, we experience what is means to be compassionate. When the needs and the pain of others break our hearts and make us weep with sorrow, it is then that, for a moment, we share in the intense and overwhelming compassion of God.

Thought for the day

For who can my fasting today make a difference?

Prayer

Lord,
show me how to fast in a way that is acceptable to you.
Help me to become more aware of the needs of others:
those close to me
and those who live in distant lands
and lead me to find some way of responding to this need
sincerely and compassionately.

Amen.

Saturday after Ash Wednesday

I have come to call sinners to repentance

Is 58:9-14; Ps 85:1-6; Lk 5:27-32

*'I have come to call not the upright but sinners
to repentance.'*

(Luke 5: 32)

I am often puzzled by this gospel reading, in which Jesus defends himself against the self-righteous Pharisees who are shocked to find him eating and drinking with tax collectors and sinners. I have always warmed to the definition of the Church as a 'community of sinners'. It makes it sound like a place where I can feel at home, knowing that we come before God as a community and as individuals in need of forgiveness and healing. We do not rejoice in our sin, but we are aware of it and accept that we all struggle to live good lives. Yet I have often felt that, with the exception of the Sacrament of Reconciliation, church is the place where it is not the done thing to even hint that one is a sinner.

The Church is meant to be a community of support and love, with no strings attached. Yet the reaction of the church community to discovering that one has sinned or done wrong in one way or another is often harsh and unforgiving. Unmarried mothers, for example, have often experienced this, in every age, in every country. In recent years, those living with HIV/AIDS have had even harsher treatment. We often find that those on the fringes of society are not accepted and welcomed. Even those who minister to marginalised individuals and groups are looked upon with suspicion. The Church proclaims a Lord who has died so that all people can be saved – yet is wary of what is 'different'.

Jesus' response to the Pharisees and their scribes is a wonderful affirmation to all of his unconditional love. He invites us – tax collectors, sinners, and self-righteous Pharisees and scribes – to enter into an open and honest relationship with him. To follow him. It seems that we sometimes forget what we have been called to do and be as Christians and have become a comfortable and self-satisfied Church. Those wonderful words of Isaiah in the first reading remind us again of what God wants from us. And, in return, God promises that our 'light will rise in the darkness' – such a beautiful image!

Thought for the day

Who do I regard as the marginalised in society? How do I treat them?

Prayer

Lord,
thank you for the unconditional love you show me.
I pray that I may be a vessel through which this love can be experienced,
especially by those who are alienated and outcast.
Help me not to judge those who are different to me
and to accept that, in you,
all people are equally valuable and beautiful.

Amen.

Imelda Davidson
First week of Lent

First Sunday of Lent

Struggling with temptation

Dt 26:4-10; Ps 90; Ro 10:8-13; Lk 4:1-13

Jesus was led by the Spirit into the desert, for forty days being put to the test by the devil.

(Luke 4:2)

In April 2000 South Africans were stunned by allegations that Hansie Cronje, captain of the national cricket team, had taken bribes for 'fixing' matches. The very idea that this national hero and role model would even contemplate doing something that was dishonest and corrupt was incomprehensible. When some of the allegations were confirmed there was a feeling of national mourning throughout the country. Public opinion was that if someone like Hansie Cronje could give in to such temptation, then anybody could.

Cronje blamed the devil for making him accept bribes to fix results. The public's reaction to this was interesting. The declaration was treated with scorn and disbelief and seen as an attempt by Cronje to shirk responsibility for his actions. In a country that has a high proportion of Christian believers there was a widespread reluctance to see Satan as a reality at work in the world.

We have all, on occasion, been faced with temptation. Many of us have succumbed to temptation, to a greater or lesser degree. I don't think that any of us could imagine the magnitude and intensity of Jesus' confrontation with

Satan in the desert. Yet these are the same kind of temptations that many people, especially those in positions of power, authority and leadership, are faced with on a daily basis. In the Church, in government, in business, in schools and in family situations, people are tempted to lord it over others, to get ahead by devious and ruthless means, to enrich themselves at the expense of the poor and needy.

Jesus was physically weak and vulnerable at the time of his testing, but he was also empowered by the Holy Spirit. The Spirit had led Jesus into the desert and, as long as he stayed rooted in his belief in God's plan for him, he would be protected and strengthened by the same Spirit. The same applies for our times of testing. We can resist temptation only by the power of the Spirit working in us.

Thought for the day

'It takes daily courage to expose oneself to God's word and to allow oneself to be judged by it.' (Dietrich Bonhoeffer)

Prayer

Lord,
you were tempted by the devil,
and yet you managed to see his empty promises for what they were.
Be with me as I face the daily temptations of life.
Let your victory over Satan inspire me to remain faithful to you and your ways.

Amen.

First Monday of Lent

Lord, when did we see you hungry or thirsty?

Lev 19:1-2, 11-18; Ps 18:8-10; Mt 25:31-46

'All nations will be assembled before him and he will separate people one from another as the shepherd separates sheep from goats.'

(Matthew 25:32)

The reading from Leviticus presents us with practical guidelines for life as relevant today as they were when they were first written. The central theme for living a good life remains essentially the same: love God and love your neighbour. This teaching from the Hebrew bible is confirmed by Jesus when he is asked, 'What must I do to inherit eternal life?' (Luke 10:27); when he is then asked, 'Who is my neighbour?' he responds with the story of the Samaritan.

In today's gospel reading from Matthew Jesus describes how at the last judgement those who recognise him in the stranger, in the person who is hungry or thirsty, in the person who is sick, are the ones who will live with him for ever.

In today's global village, we are faced with the same question: 'Who is my neighbour?' At the day of judgement we will each face the question, How did we respond to Jesus' hunger and thirst and nakedness, in the hunger, thirst and nakedness of our neighbour, our poor, oppressed, and imprisoned brother and sister in poor communities in Asia or Africa or Latin America? I imagine this might be a disturbing thought for some of those in the wealthy countries of western Europe and the United States, who often lead relatively comfortable lives.

Reflecting on life on the African continent can be a very depressing experience. There seems to be a perpetual onslaught of war, the escalation of poverty, a lack of honesty and transparency in governance, and an increase in the prevalence of HIV/AIDS. Yet, every day, ordinary people are making choices to continue to live; to celebrate life in the midst of poverty and seeming hopelessness; and choosing to take responsibility for their own and each other's lives. The western world often looks upon Africa as the poor, dependent, distant cousin, always in need, always wanting a handout; it forgets so easily that it shares in the responsibility for many of the continent's problems.

President Thabo Mbeki of South Africa has named this new century the 'African century'. His call for an African Renaissance is gradually been embraced all over the continent. Africans, together, are looking for African solutions to African problems. We are finally beginning to look at each other and recognise that we are all each other's neighbour.

Thought for the day

'True Christian worship can never let us be indifferent to the needs of others, to the cries of the hungry, of the naked and homeless, of the sick and the prisoner, of the oppressed and the disadvantaged.' (Desmond Tutu)

Prayer

Lord,
let me always be mindful of your command to love my neighbour as myself,
even when it means inconveniencing myself for the sake of others.
Help me to do small acts of kindness and goodness, without thought of reward.
Amen.

First Tuesday of Lent

The Lord's Prayer

Is 55:10-11; Ps 33:4-7, 16-19; Mt 6:7-15

'Your kingdom come, your will be done.'

(Matthew 6: 10)

The first prayer that most Christians learn by heart is the Lord's Prayer, the 'Our Father'. Yet it is often the one that we pray least from the heart. We rattle off the words from memory. Still, this is the prayer that comes automatically to the mind and tongue when we are most in need of God's help.

The Lord's Prayer is a communal prayer. It is a prayer by the community, for the community; in fact, it is a prayer for all God's people. And if we believe in the one God who created all, then it has to be a prayer for all people of all nations and all religions. When we pray 'give us this day our daily bread' we do not only pray for sustenance for Catholics, Anglicans or Protestants, or for Christians, Muslims or Jews, but for all God's people who have need of it.

Over the last few years there has been an increase in the desire for inter-religious dialogue around the world. In December 1999 Cape Town hosted the Parliament of the World's Religions. This was a wonderful celebration of the diversity of religions and spiritualities, and an unforgettable experience of tolerance and respect. I find it puzzling that while it is acknowledged that the essential tenet of all the great world religions is love of others and the call to treat others as we would have them treat us, religious difference is the most common reason (or excuse) for war. Peaceful co-existence and positive co-operation between the people of different religions sharing the same area or region can go a long way to promoting justice. Having grown up in a community where Christian, Muslim and Hindu live quite happily in harmony with one another, I know that this is possible.

As we continue our journey through Lent, let us make an effort to include those of other religions in our prayers and thoughts. Let us actively promote and practice tolerance and respect for all religions. In that way, we share in the diverse humanity that God has created.

Thought for the day

'I am part and parcel of the whole, and I cannot find God apart from the rest of humanity.' (Mahatma Gandhi)

Prayer

Lord,
help me to keep my prayers simple and sincere.
Amen.

First Wednesday of Lent

Messengers of God

Jon 3:1-10; Ps 50:3-4, 12-13, 18-19; Lk 11:29-32

*The people of Nineveh proclaimed a fast
and put on sackcloth.*

(Jonah 3:5)

The story of Jonah is a well-known and popular one. For children, the most exciting and amazing part of the story comes when Jonah is swallowed by the whale. The lesson they take from the story is that we must be obedient to God. As adults, we too find amazement in this story; amazement that upon hearing Jonah's message the whole city of Nineveh renounced the wicked things they had done and repented. God relents and lets them live.

The lesson that we learn from this story (besides that of God's endless forgiveness) is that God needs messengers and prophets to preach his word. In the gospel reading, Jesus refers to Jonah and himself as signs of God: Jonah to the Ninevites and Jesus to the people of his time. Jesus also refers to the lack of repentance of the people to whom he is preaching, and warns them of the possible condemnation that they face.

In every age, and in every time and place, God has always sent messengers and prophets to warn his people when they are in danger of breaking their covenant with him, when he sees them following the wrong paths or when they need to be reminded of his plan for them. Who are the messengers of God in our world today? Who needs to be speaking God's word to his people?

The signs of the times do not make for comfortable reading. In Africa we face a huge foreign debt burden, the destruction of our transport and communications infrastructure due to civil war and corruption, and unmanageable numbers of displaced people and refugees. Our communities are devastated by HIV/AIDS, by drug abuse and trafficking, by high levels of crime and violence. Our development is strangled by illiteracy, the oppression of women, religious fundamentalism, the weakness of our democratic structures, and the widening gap between rich and poor. Our economies are at the mercy of decisions on trade tariffs and quotas over which we have little influence.

If we, as Church, are to be God's messenger and the bearers of his good news, how do we respond to the situations that we encounter? We are often very good at expressing compassion to those who suffer – but are we prepared to challenge and change the attitudes and the systems that create and perpetuate the suffering?

Thought for the day

'There are two ways to live your life. One way is as though nothing is a miracle. The other is as though everything is a miracle.' (Albert Einstein)

Prayer

Lord,
if you have need of a messenger, I will go.
As long as you walk with me, I will go.
Even though I am afraid, I will be your sign.
Amen.

First Thursday of Lent

Women of the Word

Est 4:17; Ps 137:1-3, 7-8; Mt 7:7-12

Esther besought the Lord God of Israel in these words:
'My Lord, our King, the Only One,
come to my help, for I am alone
and have no helper but you
and am about to take my life in my hands.'

(Esther 4:17)

The story of Esther is the story of women all over the world. It is the story of all women who are deeply rooted in their relationship with God. Women who, in times of trouble, in times of danger, are able to appeal directly to the heart of God. Women who have been faithful to the laws of God. These are the women who fill our churches every week – and these are the women who shape our communities.

Esther, when faced with the annihilation of her people, risks her personal safety and status to plead for their lives. Every year in South Africa we celebrate Women's Day on 9 August. This date commemorates the march of twenty thousand women on the Union Buildings in Pretoria in 1956 to protest against the pass laws of the apartheid government. The then Prime Minister, Johannes Strydom, had previously agreed to meet with a delegation of the marchers, but when faced with this crowd of determined women, empowered and supported by each other, he was nowhere to be found. These women risked much by their actions, but were willing to pay the price for freedom from slavery.

18

Women have played a prominent and vital role in South Africa's history. It is all the more sad that we have such a high incidence of violence against women in our country. Increasing emotional, physical, sexual and economic abuse is experienced by women regardless of race, culture, religion or economic status. Our country has recently introduced new legislation, which provides for more effective protection of women, but it will take a long time before attitudes change.

Within the Church, too, we need to review the role of women, and the way in which women are regarded. For example, women are excluded from most of the decision-making in the Church, even on issues that pertain to their personal and family lives and their way of participating in the life of their own church. If the role of women in the Church is to be taken seriously, then women need to have the opportunity to tell their stories and share their experiences, so that together, men and women can come to a deeper understanding of their collaborative and mutually complementary roles.

Thought for the day
When men talk about defence, they always claim to be protecting women and children, but they never ask the women and children what they think. (Pat Schroeder)

Prayer
Lord,
help us to appreciate the beauty and strength of each woman we encounter today.
May we truly begin to understand the meaning of being created equal in your sight.
Amen.

First Friday of Lent

The peace forgiveness brings

Ezk 18:21-28; Ps 129; Mt 5:20-26

'If you are bringing your offering to the altar and there remember that your brother has something against you, leave your offering there before the altar, go and be reconciled with your brother first, and then come back and present your offering.'

(Matthew 5:23)

There is a popular story told in parish sermons about a child who awakens during the night, and, frightened by the storm outside, calls for her mother to be with her. The mother comforts her and tells her not to worry because God is with her. The child replies: 'But Mummy, I need a God with skin, that I can hold onto.'

In all of life's journeys there comes a time when, even though we believe totally in God, we desperately need to be reassured by human touch. To be comforted by human arms and to be calmed by a human voice. To feel the compassion of God made incarnate. In times of anguish and pain, in times of desolation and hopelessness, we cry for release from the depths of our hearts.

I have been volunteering as a crisis telephone counsellor for eighteen months. I have heard some of these cries. And when I cannot find the words to comfort or when the pain of people's experiences almost overwhelm me, all I can do is 'hold' them, and let them know that their cries have been heard.

When we hear the stories and experiences of people who have been hurt, abused and violated, it is hard to pray for the perpetrators, much less forgive them. We want to hurt them back; we think that they don't deserve to be prayed for. Over the past year, our city of Cape Town has experienced at least six car bomb attacks. No one has taken responsibility; there seems to be no apparent reason for these acts. People have been killed and maimed – and we're supposed to forgive those who have done this?

The peace that true forgiveness brings is not easy to achieve. The peace it brings is as much for the forgiver as for the one being forgiven. Bitterness and resentment can become ugly sores that fester in our hearts and which can perpetuate a cycle of anger and violence. The theme of forgiveness is one that is constantly explored in scripture. If our dream is to live in peace and harmony, there can be no unresolved divisions and resentments.

God forgives us, so that we may experience the liberating effects of forgiveness, both in our own lives and in the life of our community.

Thought for the day
Prayer is not asking. It is a longing of the soul. It is better in prayer to have a heart without words than words without a heart. (Mahatma Gandhi)

Prayer
Lord,
hear the cries of your people for justice and peace in our time.
Take away the pain and suffering; the war and violence.
Let joy fill our hearts once more.
Amen.

First Saturday of Lent

Love your enemies

Dt 26:16-19; Ps 118:1-2,4-5,7-8; Mt 5:43-48

*'Love your enemies and pray for those who
 persecute you.'*

(Matthew 5:44)

If this instruction of Jesus were to be taken seriously, there would be a radical change in the world as we know it today. If all those involved in conflicts, however big or small, were to look at their enemy and see, instead of 'enemy', a fellow human being: a man or woman who is part of a loving family, who desires peace, who wants a place to live and daily sustenance. If only ...

I live in South Africa, a country where 'if only' has, to a large degree, become reality. Where sworn enemies now sit down together and debate legislation for the common good, where they walk hand in hand down church aisles, sing together in church choirs, and let their children go to school together.

For those of us who lived through the 'miracle' it is hard to be blasé about the changes that have occurred. Things are very far from perfect. Racism and discrimination still exist. Negative attitudes about the 'new' South Africa are often strongly expressed. But who can deny that the winds of change have swept through the hearts of many; sometimes as a gentle breeze to lightly prod the conscience and at other times as a forceful gale, to blow into disarray old thought patterns.

Love of enemy is not just a blind acceptance that someone has changed sides and now agrees with you. It is about finding a common space, beyond the conflict, where neither is right or wrong, and beginning to dialogue about mutual interests, values and goals. It is about discovering shared hopes and dreams for a peaceful world. It is about a willingness to put aside selfish rights and talk about shared responsibilities.

This is something that happens at every level of our lives, from personal relationships to international affairs. Learning to love our enemies is about personal growth and development. It is about seeing the broader picture and recognising that we are a part of the whole and that our immediate world is not the centre of all existence. It is about being willing to sacrifice and compromise so that everybody wins.

Thought for the day

Let us trust in life because this night will pass and a new day will dawn ... let us trust in life because we do not have to live through it alone. God is with us. (Alfred Delp SJ)

Prayer

Lord,
I believe that I can make a positive difference in this world
by my attitudes and my interventions.
Help me to become more aware of the wonder, beauty and vulnerability of your creation
and to make every effort to cherish and protect it.
Amen.

David Adam
Second week of Lent

Second Sunday of Lent

The transfiguration of all

Gn 15:5-12, 17-18; Ps 26; Ph 3:17-4:1; Lk 9:28-36

They kept awake and saw his glory.

(Luke 9:32)

Here is a mountain-top experience, in a rarefied atmosphere, and yet we are called to share in it. We are all given the opportunity to be alone with Jesus and to see him for what he truly is. And in seeing him and his glory we will be changed.

Robert Browning says of the moment when he first saw his loved one: 'And suddenly life awoke.'

It was the same for the disciples. The transfiguration was not only a vision of the glory of Jesus but an awakening to what all of life is about. Vision, if it is true, always demands change within us and about us. Vision awakens us to new potential, to new ways of seeing and doing what is asked of us.

Only those who keep their eyes open are truly able to see. Many of us go through life unable to see what is about us. Jesus had purposely taken Peter, James and John with him to the mountain top. By setting them apart for a while he gave them an opportunity to see him more clearly. There is a suggestion that it was only possible for them to see Jesus and his glory if they were fully awake. They were called to be sensitive to him and all that he came to do.

Here is not only a glimpse of glory but of the one who fulfils all that the law and the prophets looked forward to. Here is a vision of humankind as it could be, how through fulfilling the law and the prophets each of us can reveal and share in the glory of God.

The glory of our Lord still waits to be revealed in much of our world. God is revealed when the laws of justice and right relationships are fulfilled. We are given a glimpse of the glory of God when freedom and righteous dealings are achieved. When slums are transfigured, when communities and peoples are redeemed from hurt and harm, when warring factions find peace, then the kingdom comes nearer to us and we reflect God's glory.

Thought for the day

'The glory of God is the human being who is fully alive to the world and all that is in it.' (St Irenaeus)

Prayer

Lord of the Transfiguration,
awaken us and we shall be changed.
Transfigure our churches, our relationships, our world;
transfigure our hopes, our dreams, our way of living.
Lord of the Transfiguration,
awaken us and we shall be changed.

Amen.

Second Monday of Lent

Fair dealing

Dn 9:4-10; Ps 78; Lk 6:36-8

*'Give, and there will be gifts for you: a full measure,
pressed down, shaken together, and running over, will
be poured into your lap; because the amount you
measure out is the amount you will be given back.'*

(Luke 6: 38)

No doubt Jesus had been watching the traders in the
market and how they dealt with people. When they sold
cloth by the arm's length, if your reach was smaller than
the trader's, they would ask you to measure it. When they
were buying, they would use their own longer arm to
make the measure. Small measures when selling, large
measures when buying. When goods were weighed on
the scales, merchants would attach a small piece of lead
under the pan with food when selling, and under the side
with weights when buying. The dealing was weighted
against the poor. Those who were unable to protect
themselves were getting short measures all the time.

We often deal in this way in everyday life, perhaps
without realising it. We use one measure for ourselves
and our friends, and another when dealing with others. It
is amazing how often we insist on tight rules for others
and yet expect total freedom for ourselves.

Our trading with the poorer nations of the third world
reflects the same double standard.

Where we can, we seek to make big profits. We measure
the success of the deal not by how fair a price we have

paid to our trading partner but by how much profit we have made. We buy for as little as we can, and we sell for as much as we can. We prefer not to think about the men and women and children who produce the goods we buy so cheaply, the long hours they work, the dangerous conditions they endure, the low wages they take home. It is easier not to ask where our bananas or our coffee come from, who grows them and harvests them.

Like the merchants who so aroused Jesus' fury, we maintain a double standard.

We have received liberally; it is right that we are liberal in our giving. Amassing wealth is not what we are on this earth for.

Thought for the day
The one who has goods and food in plenty when others have none is a robber.

Prayer
Lord,
teach us to be open-handed;
let us measure in love;
give us graciousness and generosity;
give us helpfulness and honesty;
give us fairness and friendliness;
as we have richly received, so may we richly give.

Amen.

Second Tuesday of Lent

The need for an open heart

Is 1:10, 16-20; Ps 49; Mt 23:1-12

'Take your wrongdoing out of my sight.
Cease to do evil.
Learn to do good,
search for justice,
help the oppressed,
be just to the orphan,
plead for the widow.'

(Isaiah 1:16-17)

The prophet Isaiah speaks out against religious hypocrisy, against those who attend acts of worship but ignore the will of God. Time and again in the Scriptures true worship is aligned to good relationships. I find it interesting that when our relationships with people break down so does our relationship with our God. There can be no right relationship with God if we have bad relationships with other people.

When we ignore or abuse any part of God's creation we ignore and abuse our God. It is no use rejoicing in Creation if we continue to carelessly pollute our world. If we rape and pillage the earth, even if it is far from our backyard, our relationship with the Creator has broken down. God's kingdom cannot come on the earth if we are careless in our dealings with our neighbours or with the planet. Let the Church never be silent where lives are at risk or people are belittled. We are all part of the body of Christ. We cannot say that what we do in private does not hurt anybody for what we do influences our whole lives and the lives of those around us.

When one member of a family suffers the whole family suffers. When one member of a community is neglected the whole of that community is impoverished. As long as there are communities and families in need, wherever they are in the world, we are all called to help meet their needs. To ignore the cry of the oppressed is to allow part of the God-like image in us to die.

It is easy to feel overwhelmed by cries of help from all around the world. It is tempting to ignore the appeals for people suffering because of floods or famine or war. There seem to be so many emergencies, so many charities worthy of our support. We must not let the fact that we cannot do everything be an excuse for doing nothing. Where we can be of use we should make ourselves available. It is in meeting the needs of others that we so often are met by the great Other who is God.

Thought for the day

Join a good cause; you may not be able to do much for it but it will do a lot for you.

Prayer

Lord our God,
you call us in the poor and the needy,
you speak to us through the cries of the oppressed,
you ask us to share in your work of redemption and healing:
make us worthy of this calling;
through Jesus Christ our Lord.

Amen.

Second Wednesday of Lent

Called to serve

Jr 18:18-20; Ps 30; Mt 20:17-28

'Anyone who wants to be great among you must be your servant, and anyone who wants to be first among you must be your slave, just as the Son of Man came not to be served but to serve and to give up his life as a ransom for many.'

(Matthew 20: 26-28)

So often the Christian way turns the way of the world upside down. When the world seeks to possess, Jesus says, 'It is more blessed to give'. We learn that true riches are measured not in what we possess but in what we are able to give away: the rich person is the one who is able to give with joy.

This is true not only of money but of time and service. The worldly seek to be served by others, whereas Christians are asked to be willing to spend their lives in serving and in caring for people. In a strange way those who do this find they are enriched. It is by losing our lives in service that we gain the life that is eternal. Time and again in this life we learn that it is in giving that we receive in good measure.

In today's gospel reading the disciples are trying to work out a fair return for what they are doing. Like all of us they have ambitions and hope to rise in the eyes of the world, to hold a position of authority and to be looked up to. They want a profit out of their giving. They are still learning that any position brings responsibility and the higher the position the greater the responsibility. They want to rule but Jesus wants them to serve. The disciples have to discover that true greatness is not in dominating but in serving, not in seeking to make people do what we want but in being willing to meet them and their needs without costing it out.

The disciples were making their demands after Jesus had talked of the ultimate sacrifice. He had been talking of his impending capture, condemnation and crucifixion. While Jesus speaks of laying down his life, the disciples want to talk about the Kingdom that he will be ruler of. Either this shows great faith in Jesus or they are not listening to what he is saying. Knowing human frailty, it was probably a mixture of both.

We want the crown but we would rather avoid the cross. We seek the benefits of belief but we would rather ignore its demands. Following in the steps of our Saviour we need to remember that he was willing to give his life even to death to win back people to God. Our limited giving and our limited serving cause a great weakness in the Church.

Thought for the day

The richest person is not the one with possessions but the one who dares give away the most.

Prayer

Teach us good Lord to serve you as you deserve:
to give and not to count the cost,
to fight and not to heed the wounds,
to toil and not to seek for rest,
to labour and not to ask for any reward,
save that of knowing that we do your will.

Amen.

Second Thursday of Lent

God who comes in the Other

Jr 17:5-10; Ps 1; Lk 16:19-31

'There was a rich man who used to dress in purple and fine linen and feast magnificently every day. And at his gate there used to lie a poor man called Lazarus, covered with sores, who longed to fill himself with what fell from the rich man's table.'

(Luke 16:19-21)

The story of the rich man and the poor man is a great warning about the dangers of insensitivity. The point of the story is not that the rich man was said to be wicked; no doubt he kept the law and attended the synagogue on the Sabbath. The rich man did not move Lazarus on, he did not kick him, he did not pass judgement on him. In fact he did not do anything towards him. And it is for this that the rich man is condemned – he did not even notice the poor man. He was unaware. He was insensitive to Lazarus. This reminds me of the poster that said, 'Forget the hungry and they will go away – and die.'

It is costly to be sensitive. To be blind allows us not to see the injustice of the systems we live by, so that we can feel comfortable and secure. To be deaf allows us not hear the cry of the poor, so that we can keep our possessions to ourselves. To have our eyes and ears opened can make great demands upon us, and cause us much pain. But if we are to be fully human our ears and eyes have to be used as well as we can use them. To turn a blind eye or a deaf ear is not an option for a follower of Christ. To harden our hearts is to allow part of ourselves to die. What does it benefit us to gain the whole world and lose our own soul?

The rich man is condemned not for his riches but for his insensitivity, his blindness, his deafness. There is nothing wrong in having possessions. But those with riches have a responsibility to those who have none.

The story concludes with the rich man in hell, asking if a special message of warning might be sent to his brothers. The reply, though sounding harsh, is a warning to us all. Perhaps we are the rich man's brothers and sisters. Jesus says if we do not heed the law and the prophets neither will we be persuaded though one who rose from the dead. It would seem that insensitivity in one area, such as in our relationships with the poor, allows insensitivity to grow in other areas, such as the Scriptures, and even our relationship with the risen Lord.

Thought for the day

'We cannot know whether we love God, although there may be strong reasons for thinking so, but there can be no doubt whether we love our neighbour or not. Be sure that in proportion as you advance in brotherly love, you increase in your love of God.' (St Teresa of Avila)

Prayer

Open our eyes to your presence and to the people around us.
Open our ears to your call and to the cry of the needy.
Open our hearts to your love and to all who call for love from us:
that we may be fully alive and serve you in others;
through Christ our Lord.

Amen.

Second Friday of Lent

Call to the fruit producers

Gn 37:3-4, 12-13, 17-28; Ps 104; Mt 21:33-43, 45-46

'I tell you that the kingdom of God will be taken from you and given to a people who will produce its fruit.'

(Matthew 21:43)

I have a fear of groups that are able to talk about work rather than do it. Sometimes a committee is a good way of avoiding getting anything done. Some churches are in danger of living in this way. It is no use talking about the world or the area we live in unless we are willing to take action upon our discoveries and debates. Our prayers demand that we also say, 'Your will be done in and through us'. In our awareness of the inequalities of the world, of poverty and injustice, we are called to act. We may need to talk, we may need meetings, but in the end we are called to act to produce the fruits of our thoughts and our prayers.

In the parable of the wicked tenants, they are condemned for their attitude to the land. They lived in the vineyard as if it belonged to them and they owed nothing to anyone. Long before these people arrived on the scene the landowner had prepared a good land for them. He had planted it, fenced it round, dug a winepress and built a tower. The tenants were given all these riches to enjoy while the owner was abroad.

It is important to note that the land is leasehold. The tenants are only given use of it for a time. In return the landowner expects to be able to collect the fruit. Trees and tenants that do not produce are useless. These tenants gained riches from the land but assumed that it was theirs to keep and do with it as they wished. They fought to keep it to themselves. They set up a protectionist policy to keep all claimants away. They would not listen, they beat, stoned and killed anyone who came asking for a share. If they did this to agents of the landowner they would no doubt have had a go at the tenant himself and ejected or killed him if they could. It is amazing how many of us have protected ourselves against the call of God.

Remember that when God sent his Son, 'He came to his own domain and his own people did not accept him' (John 1:11). The very Son of God became the scorned and rejected of men. He was put to death on a cross. If you go back to Genesis you discover the crucifixion begins when we disobey God and use the earth and its produce as we please without recourse to the Creator and owner.

God does not exclude anyone but we exclude ourselves from his love by our actions and attitude towards him and towards others.

Thought for the day

The earth does not belong to us, we belong to the earth and all belongs to God.

Prayer

Lord,
restore to us a gentleness of touch;
give us a sensitivity towards our world;
give us an awareness of our dealings with others;
give us a willingness to share what we have received
and make us hospitable to all who come to us.
Amen.

Second Saturday of Lent

Knowing when you are lost

Mi 7:14 -15, 18-20; Ps 102; Lk 15:1-3, 11-32

*'He was angry then and refused to go in, and his father
came out to plead with him.'*

(Luke 15:28)

Three parables of God's mercy are told because of the
'righteousness' of the Pharisees and scribes. These good
people objected to Jesus eating with 'sinners'. It would
seem their goodness prevented them from discovering
the deep love of God for all his people.

In the story of the Prodigal Son we miss the whole
point if we concentrate on the waywardness of the
Prodigal. The younger son, who was lost because of his
own foolishness, at least knew of his father's love; the
Prodigal was sure of forgiveness and acceptance. He
had been lost and knew it, but now he was found
again. The older son found this situation intolerable
and said so. This good man lived by the law and
believed that everyone who did not live by his
standards should be punished. There is a hardness
about those who live by the law alone. Life is tough if
you do not know how to act out of love. The older son's
sternness separated him from the father and his love; it
would not allow him to join in the celebrations on the
return of the Prodigal. It is the older son who is truly
lost. The younger one found his way home; the older
one had to be sought out by the father.

It always amazes me when people refuse to help a good cause with the words, 'They should help themselves. They are in this plight from their own foolishness. If we give them money they will just waste it. They do not deserve help.' Some will only help those who agree with their standards or conditions. I recently met a priest who said he only helped Christians. I really wonder how he measured this. God offers his love and his help to all people and he asks us to do the same.

The hardest people to help are those who do not know that they are lost. It is difficult to give anything to those who believe they have 'earned' their position – and 'earned' God's love and grace. Those who feel they have earned what they have do not yet know of the deep love of God as shown in the cross and the crucifixion of our Lord. God's grace can only be given to those who open themselves to this free gift of himself. Know that if we are outside, our God comes out to be where we are.

Thought for the day

There is no one outside the love of God except those who place themselves there.

Prayer

Lord,
you seek out all who are lost, all who are weary, all who are heavily burdened;
you seek out the foolish and the sinner,
you seek such as me.
Lord, may I open my life to your love,
may I open my heart to your grace
and my days to your presence;
through Christ our risen and ascended Lord
who is alive and reigns with you and the Holy Spirit,
one God, for ever and ever.

Amen.

Margaret Hebblethwaite
Third week of Lent

Third Sunday of Lent

Just looking

Ex 3:1-8, 13-15; Ps 102; 1 Cor 10:1-6,10-12; Lk 13:1-9

The angel of Yahweh appeared to Moses in a flame blazing from the middle of a burning bush.

(Exodus 3:2)

Alone in the countryside we can see natural sights of amazing, even fiery beauty, as we watch the sun rise, or the sun set. The blaze of the golden ball of flame, which spreads its fingers of light over the sea and across the clouds, can remind us of Moses' burning bush, where the holy presence of God was found. We fall naturally into silence and awe as we watch the slowly changing fire. This is the basis of contemplation, or as it is sometimes known, the 'prayer of simple regard', that is, the prayer of just looking.

Our attention is caught by the beauty of the fire, and then we let our mind move to the creator of the beauty. It is as though God speaks a little louder to us at dawn and at sunset. The vision is a powerful one, and just as Moses covered his eyes, afraid to look at God, so too we may need to shield our eyes against the strength of the sun when it rises in the morning and breaks through its covering of clouds.

What is God's message at these times of silence and awe?

First, it is a message of awareness of the daily struggle of life. As surely as the sun sheds light on all, so God knows of the sufferings of those who work hard for little or no reward. God knows how much we need simple good things, the 'milk and honey' of life, nourishment and sweetness, without breaking ourselves in the process. This is a God who dissolves stress and restores a sense of dignity and freedom.

Second, it is a message of ultimate and universal reality. This may be the God of Abraham, Isaac and Jacob, but the divine nature goes deeper than any culture or race. Though we may speak of 'Yahweh', or 'Allah', or 'God', there is a divine name deeper and beyond our words. This is based simply on the first person present of the verb 'to be', in any language: 'I am who I am', the ground of all being and the heart of all meaning.

Thought for the day

We can never destroy the sun or put out its light, but we can cast a curtain of smog and pollution between us and this source of life and beauty.

Prayer

O God, you are compassion and love.
Standing before you, barefoot in spirit if not in body,
I try to open my heart to your values.
Help me to see the miserable state of your people,
to hear their appeal to be free,
and to do my part in bringing milk and honey to your children.

Amen.

Third Monday of Lent

Foolish comparisons

2 K 5:1-15; Ps 41-42; Lk 4:24-30

Elisha sent Naaman a message to say,
'Go and bathe seven times in the Jordan,
and your flesh will become clean.'

(2 Kings 5: 10)

'Surely the rivers of Damascus are better than any water in Israel?' We all have had thoughts along these lines, particularly when we are far from home and missing the security of our own country. Surely academic standards are better in England than in the remote islands of the Pacific? Surely the trained voices of Wales are of a higher quality than the primitive, throaty voices of peasants in Latin America? Surely British scientific expertise can be trusted more than the haphazard technology of the South?

The trouble with making these comparisons is that we are not always comparing like with like. A student with high academic standards may make foolish and distorted judgements. Music may be polished and practised and yet lack the depth of feeling of someone who sings from the heart. British water, in spite of the thoroughness of the purification and filtering systems, never tastes as good as a cup of water in a hot country where clean water is the poor person's gold.

Comparing 'better' and 'worse' is most sinister in a place where there is racial tension or even violent confrontation. Whether the land is Northern Ireland or Rwanda or Fiji, there will be no healing for anyone on either side so long as people promote the idea that 'our water is purer than theirs', or 'our culture is richer than theirs'.

The biblical message, despite its roots in the story of the Jewish people, so often challenges this sort of cultural one-upmanship. Elisha was a Jewish prophet, but the leper he healed was Syrian. Ruth was a Moabite, but she became the foremother of Jesse and David and Jesus. Jesus was a Galilean, but the people of his village tried to throw him off the cliff when he told them 'no prophet is ever accepted in his own country'.

Only when political tensions flare do we realise how important is the obvious message that racism or narrow nationalism is wrong. We all love and favour our own country, but if we do not learn to love and favour other people's cultures as a regular habit we will not be ready with the seeds of peace when they are really needed.

Thought for the day

Naaman could not buy his health cure. He could only be cured by divesting himself of what he had, even his clothes, and immersing himself as though seeking forgiveness through baptism.

Prayer

I will ask for healing from you, O God,
from whatever is my personal sickness.
I will accept the conditions you place for granting me health,
even if they seem ridiculously easy.
Then I will come to the altar of God with thanksgiving,
the God of my joy.
Amen.

Third Tuesday of Lent

The most acceptable offering

Dn 3:25, 34-43; Ps 24; Mt 18:21-35

They walked in the heart of the flames, praising God and blessing the Lord.

(Daniel 3:25)

Shadrach, Meshach and Abed-Nego were three young Jewish men thrown into a fiery furnace for refusing to worship the golden statue set up by King Nebuchadnezzar of Babylon. The king was amazed to see that they were not burned but walked freely in the heart of the flames. There even seemed to be a fourth person, presumed to be an angel, walking alongside them.

The Old Testament reading for today is the prayer of Abed-Nego, whose Hebrew name was Azariah. But though it is spoken from an extreme situation, from the heart of the flames, it has lasting and universal relevance. He is saying that in their situation of dire need they are in absolute poverty and have nothing to offer at all – no sacrifice, no incense, no one to lead their prayer. And yet they have a desperately important prayer to make: a plea for deliverance. It is because of their total poverty that they are driven to offer the only thing they have, a contrite soul and a humble spirit, in the hope that it will be as acceptable to God as thousands of fattened lambs or rams or bullocks.

In fact, we know from Scripture that a contrite soul and a humble spirit is far more acceptable to God than any number of animal sacrifices. Azariah's poverty, in that moment of crisis, has driven him to discover the most important truth of all, that God cares about the intentions of the heart far more than about material offerings. You cannot buy God, you can only win God by purity of intention. As the Psalmist said: 'The sacrifice acceptable to God is a broken spirit; a broken and contrite heart, O God, you will not despise' (Psalm 51:17).

So the poor are at no disadvantage when it comes to making their peace with God. On the contrary, their poverty prepares them to be more aware of their need of God, and more open to God's will. We all know how readily we turn to God when we are desperate, and how easily we forget God when life is going smoothly.

Thought for the day

Today's gospel warns that God will punish forgiven debtors if they do not pass on to others the forgiveness they have received. This is a warning to Christian nations who are still holding poor countries responsible for unpaid debts.

Prayer

Teach me your paths, O God,
and make me walk in your truth.
May the flames of temptation that lick around my feet
be as harmless to me as the furnace in which the
Hebrew children were thrown.
Let me walk among the world's dangers without fear
as I place my trust in you.

Amen.

Third Wednesday of Lent

Set in stone

Dt 4:1, 5-9; Ps 147; Mt 5:17-19

*'Do not imagine I have come to abolish the Law
or the Prophets. I have come not to abolish
but to complete them.'*

(Matthew 5: 17)

Jesus was never dismissive of the Law. Moses speaks with great pride of the Law that he has brought from God to the people: 'What great nation is there that has laws and customs to match this whole Law that I put before you today?'

It is easy to undermine the Law in the name of a higher rule of the spirit. But when we are under pressure we realise just how precious the Ten Commandments are. They can sound so obvious that we think they are not worth repeating. But then we find ourselves faced by people who call themselves Christian and yet breach these rules, and we realise what an infinitely precious resource it is to have the obvious set down in stone.

'You shall have no other gods.' Yet theologians like Jon Sobrino of El Salvador have pointed out how the gods of money and political power have become the idols of our modern age, justifying any law-breaking.

'You shall not make wrongful use of the name of God.' Yet the fight against so-called 'communists' has driven paramilitary groups to murder, rape, lie and steal, all in the name of Christianity.

'Keep holy the Sabbath.' Yet the sanctuary of the church has been broken and the Blessed Sacrament has been scattered over the ground, in anger vented against the local congregation.

'Honour your father and your mother.' Yet the elderly are often forgotten by young people too busy to show a basic debt of gratitude to those who brought them into the world.

'You shall not murder.' These were the words of Archbishop Romero in his famous last sermon, when he begged the soldiers to remember that God's Law was a higher command than that of their officers. For this reminder of the Ten Commandments, he paid with his own life.

Moses tells us not to be cowed into silence about the Law of God. The commandments are something to be handed down with pride 'to your children and to your children's children' (Deuteronomy 4:9).

Thought for the day

We carve words in stone on gravestones to make the point that the life of our loved ones is so precious that death can never wipe out their memory. God's Law is as precious as that.

Prayer

Help me to find the best way
to pass on your commands to my children,
and to my children's children,
so that they may repeat them and treasure them,
observe them and love them,
and that following them they may have the light of life.
Amen.

Third Thursday of Lent

A sign of life

Jr 7:23-28; Ps 94; Lk 11:14-23

O that today you would listen to his voice!
Harden not your hearts as at Meribah.

(Psalm 94:7)

The psalmist's refrain is familiar. But what actually happened at Meribah?

In Exodus 17 we are told how the Israelites suddenly turned against Moses because they were thirsty. They said, 'Is God among us or not?' and they even accused Moses of doing the wrong thing in freeing them from their slavery.

'Why did you bring us out of Egypt, to kill us and our children and livestock with thirst?' they cried, and they were ready to stone him in their frustration.

But God was still looking after the people and provided water through another miracle at Meribah. Moses struck the rock with his staff and water came out of it so that the people could drink. The people earned no credit for their faithlessness and ingratitude, but Meribah went down in Jewish memory as a token of divine providence.

Drinking water is still a desperate need for millions of people on the earth. Streams and wells are often polluted, giving people dysentery or worms. Those who travel to developing countries are gravely warned against drinking local water, unless they have checked that is healthy, or unless they have treated it with iodine or chlorine tablets, or boiled it.

So Meribah with its spring of water is a powerful symbol of God's goodness, assuring us that God provides for our needs. Water is a sign of life, in more ways than one: it quenches our thirst, makes the plants grow, and washes us clean. No wonder that baptism uses water as its key symbol. But turning on a tap in Europe has become so easy that we often forget how precious water is.

Meribah is a symbol but it is also more than a symbol. It is a reminder that God wants people to have water, not just symbolically, but actually. When we do something towards helping people to have good, clean drinking water, we are sharing in the life-giving action of the good and loving God.

Thought for the day

Habit is such an insistent force that people will often choose to go back to old enslavements after they have once been freed, because they feel more at home there.

Prayer

Help me to listen to your voice, O God.
Do not let me be overcome by anger and frustration,
or by the desire to revert to habits that enslave me.
You have done so much for me already
that I should know you will go on leading me
to health and freedom, if I go on following you.
Amen.

Third Friday of Lent

Love is ...

Hos 14:-10; Ps 80; Mk 12:8-34

'You must love the Lord your God with all your heart, with all your soul, with all your mind and with all your strength ... You must love your neighbour as yourself.'

(Mark 12:30-31)

Today's gospel reading gives us the two greatest commandments, which implicitly contain all the rest of the Law.

'Love' is not just a woolly idea, an empty word that easily trips off the tongue. A passionate, all-consuming, kind of love is demanded. It is so complete that four phrases are used to reinforce and drive home the meaning of the love God asks of us: love with all your heart, love with all your soul, love with all your mind, love with all your strength.

Today's first reading, from Hosea, develops lovely nature imagery to illustrate what it means when God says, 'I will love them with all my heart.' In an industrial society we tend to forget the sights and smells of nature, but for a rural people the words are full of memory and resonance.

Love is like dew falling, says God, moist and life-giving, the night's gift to the coming day. Love is like the lily blooming, a brilliant flash of white beauty, fragile and pure. Love is like the roots of the poplar, thrusting out so deep and far that the person who loves becomes a source of unshakable strength to others. Love is like the olive for its loveliness, and it has the fragrance of Lebanon, an area famed for its cedars, wines and cool waters.

So love has both the security of a firmly rooted tree, and the delicate perfume of a fragile flower. It has both the fresh coolness of morning dew, and the rich warmth of olives with their oil. Such is the love God has for us. And such is the love of the whole heart and soul and mind and strength that God can inspire in us. This love, the gospel tells us, echoing Tuesday's message, is 'far more important than any holocaust or sacrifice'.

In the imagery of Hosea, this is the love in which people rest as though in a fertile land, where corn and vines flourish. Corn and vines, of course, are the source of the bread and wine of the eucharist, the ultimate sign of love between God and humanity.

Thought for the day

Love calls forth love. The more we understand how much God loves us, the more we find we love God in return, without effort or straining.

Prayer

You are the God who brought your people out of the land of Egypt.
In my life, too, there has been an Egypt from which you have delivered me.
Only you and I know quite what is meant by that, for enslavement and liberation are a very personal matter.
Thank you for what you have done for me, and keep me free for ever.
Amen.

Third Saturday of Lent

The perfect prayer

Hos 5:15-6:6; Ps 50; Lk 18:9-14

'Everyone who raises himself up will be humbled, but anyone who humbles himself will be raised up.'

(Luke 18:14)

In the parable of the Pharisee and the tax collector, Jesus tells us the words of their secret prayers. But we can tell a great deal just from their body language. We can easily imagine the two men in the temple, the one standing confidently and somewhat smugly, the other hovering in the background, lowering his eyes and quietly beating his breast. We have to remember that being a tax collector was considered a grave sin in itself, for it was a form of collusion with the Roman occupation. People did not become tax collectors out of conviction, but because they loved money more than their reputation.

So this is not a story of a 'good man' and a 'bad man'. On the contrary, the Pharisee lived in a way that was genuinely virtuous. He was not greedy or grasping. He was not unjust or dishonest. He was not involved in sexual sins. What is more, he used to fast, not just once a week but twice. Not many of us do that. And he paid tithes on all the money he earned. Not many of us can say that, either.

Yet one thing spoiled all the Pharisee's good works: pride. And all the weakness and greed of the tax collector was made up for by one thing: the sincerity with which he asked for forgiveness. His prayer, 'God be merciful to me a sinner', is a prayer so perfect that it has become the heart of the famous Jesus prayer used by the Orthodox: 'Jesus Christ, son of the living God, have mercy on me, a sinner.'

Jesus tells us, over and over again, in all sorts of ways, how God wants us to be humble. 'Blessed are the meek', he says, 'for they shall inherit the earth' (Matthew 5:5). And, 'whoever becomes humble like this child is the greatest in the kingdom of heaven' (Matthew 18:4).

In a world divided between over-confident, self-righteous people – mostly, though not entirely, from the powerful, economically successful countries – and humble, simple people – largely, though not exclusively, from the impoverished regions – we know who has the greater need to make their peace with God.

Thought for the day

Jesus favours the people who cannot walk straight or speak out. He helps the bent-over woman to stand up, and the dumb man to find his voice, liberating them from their bodily inhibitions.

Prayer

A humble, contrite heart you will not spurn, O God.
Teach me never to compare myself favourably with someone else I regard as a sinner,
for you alone know the secret prayers of the heart.
If I succeed in serving you,
do not let me forget that I do so by your strength,
for on my own account I can achieve nothing.

Amen.

Charles Hedley
Fourth week of Lent

Fourth Sunday of Lent

A world in change

Jos 5:9, 10-12; Ps 34:2-3, 4-5, 6-7; 2 Co 5:17-21; Lk 15:1-3, 11-32

So if anyone is in Christ, there is a new creation: everything old has passed away; see, everything has become new!

(2 Corinthians 5:17)

With the collapse of the former communist regimes in Europe and the end of the cold war politicians began to talk about the 'new world order'. The changed world would not be dominated by a confrontation between two rival political ideologies. There would be a greater sense of the importance of human rights and shared responsibilities, and more powerful international bodies such as the United Nations. Today, however, we still have the same old order, but with different players. We are still far from achieving a shared sense of belonging to the same world, and to one another.

In his second letter to the church in Corinth Paul wrote that the new order was not to come about through human achievement, but is already present when a person is 'in Christ'. Those who make their own what God has already achieved for us belong to the new creation. Paul's talk of 'new creation' echoes the original creation stories in the Bible and recalls the idea of God's original blessing. In Genesis God blesses all living beings in creation and sees that this creation is very good. The discovery 'in Christ' of our belonging to one another, and of all of us belonging to God, replaces the sense of 'I on my own' and opens us to new possibilities.

The old order, which Paul tells us has passed away, consists of the whole world of relationships constituted by selfishness, by love of power, and by greed. We still live in a world which, in many ways, expresses the old order. Our lives still contain much which is unchanged. We can, however, decide to change the direction of our lives, to live on the basis of faith. We can step into the new world and, prophetically, live in the 'new order'.

In the midst of the old creation, our lives can express the new creation of grace, generosity and a sense of solidarity with the poor. Just as the Israelites crossed into the promised land and took possession of it and enjoyed its produce, so those who live by grace take possession of the new creation.

Thought for the day

The new creation does not start with us and our efforts. It has already started in Christ.

Prayer

Creator God,
you call us to be made anew
and to live in a world renewed.
In the midst of the old world
may we live prophetically
the life of your new creation.

Amen.

Fourth Monday of Lent

New heavens and a new earth

Is 65:17-21; Ps 30:2, 4, 5-6, 11-13; Jn 4:43-54

They shall build houses and inhabit them; they shall plant vineyards and eat their fruit.

(Isaiah 65:21)

Isaiah describes his vision of the new heavens and the new earth. He writes of a world where weeping is a thing of the past; where children do not die in infancy; and where houses, food and health are found in abundance. It is not an imaginary Utopia of the spirit lying beyond space and time, but a real world – the world of our human history.

In today's world the poor are often unjustly deprived of the fruits of their labour. Every day an estimated 19,000 children die in developing nations as a result of resources being diverted from health and education to servicing debts to rich countries. The US pastor, Jim Wallis, has written that the issue is not, What will we give to the poor? It is, When will we stop taking from the poor?'

The 'second sign' – Jesus's second miracle in Cana of Galilee – is the healing of a little child who was at death's door. Jesus tells the father, 'Your child will live'. The child restored to a full life is a sign and a fulfilment of the vision of new heavens and a new earth. The miracle comes from faith met with blessing by God. 'You have changed my mourning into dancing' (Psalm 30:11).

The gift of life must be received, nurtured and valued. We fear justice, we imagine that if the poor are to be enriched we will 'lose' something. We do not understand that justice is the necessary foundation for a flourishing of the whole world, ourselves included.

Isaiah speaks with the voice of the poor. He writes of hope for a beaten people, of change that is God's creating but which is expressed through human action. When we work with the poor to reverse the catastrophe of poverty in human life, we find real joy and delight. It is God's creating, but it is our doing, and we may find ourselves being the ones who are transformed.

Thought for the day
The kingdom is God's project in history and eternity.

Prayer
O God of rich and poor alike,
you create a world of interdependence.
Help us to see how the thirst for your justice
not only helps the poor,
and puts right a tilted world,
but changes us
and makes us new.
Amen.

Fourth Tuesday of Lent

Waters of life

Ezk 47:1-9, 12; Ps 45; Jn 5:1-3, 5-16.

Their leaves will not wither nor their fruit fail, but they will bear fresh fruit every month because the water for them flows from the sanctuary.

(Ezekiel 47:12)

Arriving in a small oasis in the Sahara Desert, I encountered the men of the village all seated around the well. We did not speak, but their first action was to draw from the well a great plastic beaker of water. This was passed around for each of us to drink from. Only when we had quenched our thirst did they greet me. The real welcome, however, was in their invitation to drink with them. It was an act of communion – the sharing of a common cup – but it also ensured my survival in the great heat of that day.

Water can symbolise many things, but essentially it is simply what is needed for life. Development projects to dig new wells in sub-Saharan Africa are not symbols. They are the raw reality of survival. In his vision, as Ezekiel wades deeper into the water, he becomes more aware of the life that it provides: the fish within it, the plants which grow beside it and which owe their very life to it. The very coolness of the water expresses its reviving power.

The river in the vision symbolises that all life and hope find their origin in God, but flow out to us, bringing healing and renewal. For Ezekiel, heaven is conceived as a place on earth. It is the point where God and the lives of human beings intersect. It is God who comes to dwell with us, not the other way round, and where God is found, there you will find all the qualities that you find in heaven. The earth is transformed to a land of abundance, where the waters of life flow and cleanse and purify the land and the people. God becomes the well-spring of life for the people.

Ezekiel expresses the reality of God's blessings. What we receive from God is not for us alone, but is to be shared out for all the people, rich and poor alike. These blessings may be expressed through simple acts of solidarity with the poor, signing a petition to drop the debt, or making a donation on family fast day. They may be expressed through listening to our family and friends and colleagues and responding with respect. Or they may be expressed through learning from people whose faith or culture differ from our own, and using their insights to enlarge our own vision. When these things happen we may well find that we are the ones who receive the blessings.

Thought for the day
God is the Creator, and we are made in God's likeness and image to be co-creators.

Prayer
Creator God,
we give you thanks
for the gift of water
through which we are revived and refreshed.
May the living water of your Spirit
renew our energies and our imagination,
and admit us to the new world
where our spirits are yours
and our struggles are yours also.
Amen.

Fourth Wednesday of Lent

Acting visibly

Is 49:8-15; Ps 145: 8-9, 13-14, 17-18; Jn 5:17-30

'Can a woman forget her nursing child, or show no compassion for the child of her womb? Even these may forget, but I will not forget you.'

(Isaiah 49:15)

The sense of patience and continuing love in God's dealings with humanity is shown in both today's reading from Isaiah and in today's gospel. God's love for us, and in particular for those who experience hopelessness, is greater even than that of a mother for her child.

The servant (whoever that might be) is given authority to speak and behave differently, so that those in prison and those whose lives are diminished may find freedom. If you trust in God you become able to live in a way which changes the world. God changes us and gives us power to act – even though in ourselves we might feel completely at a loss. The call to 'show yourselves' is a call for us to 'be visible' – to begin to exist again.

Jesus acted very visibly in healing on the Sabbath and in making known God's power even though it upset the established order. It is a sign of his authority over all things. Were we made for the Sabbath, or was the Sabbath made for us? Which comes first – the real needs of people or the trading systems and employment laws under which we live? The international order is not God-given. We have developed it for ourselves. And we can change it for ourselves.

Isaiah wrote at the time of the return from exile – the 'time of God's favour'. Rather as the land had been shared out when the people had first arrived, now it would be re-apportioned for the returning exiles, as everyone needed some land in order to plant their crops and bring forth a harvest. Isaiah looked to a time when God's original blessing would be restored – when the land would yield its produce and when there would be justice and fair-dealing for all.

How will this transformation come about? Jesus supplies the answer in the way he faces those who were looking to kill him. He was aware that he could do nothing on his own, but that in seeking to do God's will, everything would be achieved. 'The hour is coming, and is now here, when the dead will hear the voice of the Son of God, and those who hear will live.' Even the dead were not beyond his reach. Even those whose lives seem completely lost can be transformed through the life that comes from God.

Thought for the day

The rights of the poor are God's rights.

Prayer

O God,
you call us into existence,
and give us authority to act.
Enable us to follow the example of Jesus
and to live and act
only through the power and authority
which comes from being obedient
to your will.

Amen.

Fourth Thursday of Lent

Image and reality

Ex 32:7-14; Ps 106:19-20, 21-22, 23; Jn 5:31-47

They fashioned a calf at Horeb and worshipped an image of metal, exchanging the God who was their glory for the image of a bull that eats grass.

(Psalm 106: 19-20)

The people of Israel were afraid that they had lost Moses. He had gone up to the mountain and had not yet returned. It was a difficult time for them. They had made the perilous journey out of Egypt, but had not yet entered the promised land. They were already breaking the promise they had made 'not to make any graven image'. Canaan was unknown to them and they did not know who they would find there. The bull was a symbol of the fertility that was required of the land if they were to settle there and flourish.

But their new god was not even a pale reflection of the God who had led them out of Egypt and given them their freedom. A grass-eating ox can in no way compare with 'the God who was their glory'. They were worshipping something that they had made. They had replaced the creator of the world and everything in it, with an idol which they could control. Their god was too small – because their god was no real god at all.

Today our idols take other forms. We still look to images, but the images which seduce us now are the images presented by the media – celebrity, advertising and political 'spin'. Like the golden calf of the Israelites our substitutes for God not only fall short of the original – they fall spectacularly short. We wear the 'right' clothes, eat the 'right' food, and make the shape of our bodies conform to the fashion of the day. We deny the worth that lies within us, which comes from being a human being created in the image of God. As Jesus says in today's gospel: 'How can you believe when you accept glory from one another and do not seek the glory that comes from the one who alone is God?' (John 5:44).

It was partly fear which had made the Israelites pander to their new god. They were afraid because Moses seemed to have abandoned them and they faced an unknown future in Canaan. When we act out of fear we look for help, support, strength and encouragement wherever we can find it. There is a striking contrast here with Jesus' teaching that the poor are blessed because they know their need of God. We are invited not to be conformed to this world out of fear but to find the love of God which banishes fear and gives us the strength to be truly who we are and to live and act in the truth.

Thought for the day

The opposite of love is not hatred, it is fear. Perfect love banishes fear.

Prayer

O God of all the peoples on earth,
may love flow into our hearts
and fear flow out.

Amen.

Fourth Friday of Lent

Truth sets us free

Ws 2:1, 12-22; Ps 34:17-18, 19-20, 21, 23; Jn 7:1-2,10,25-30

Is not this the man whom they are trying to kill?
And here he is, speaking openly,
but they say nothing to him!

(John 7:25)

To stand up and speak out takes courage. There are always those (as in today's reading from the book of Wisdom) who say, 'Let us lie in wait for those who are righteous, because they are inconvenient to us and oppose our actions.' Those who campaign for justice for the poor, or for a change in the political order, are not pushing at an open door. Justice for the poor is going to be 'inconvenient' for those who benefit from their exploitation. There will always be scoffers and fair weather friends. Jubilee 2000's campaign to wipe out unpayable debts owed by third world countries has not marched 'from glory to glory'.

The gospel reading tells us of the people who see Jesus and ask: 'How is it that the Pharisees are trying to kill Jesus, but when he speaks openly in the temple they say nothing to him?' Jesus had found safety through speaking in the temple, through going out only in daylight and visiting places where a crowd was present. He was protected to some extent because of the way he chose to operate – not by plotting or scheming but by speaking out boldly. It was a risky course of action. When he deliberately chose to go out at night to the isolated garden, his enemies moved in and arrested him.

We now live in a shrinking, interdependent world. It is more difficult for corrupt regimes to suppress voices of opposition from within or to ignore voices of protest from without. Multinational companies have been forced to withdraw investments in countries such as Burma because of their fear of losing customers. Amnesty International has brought about the easing of conditions of prisoners of conscience – and even effected their release – through bringing their plight to the light of day. Just by speaking the truth, by telling the story, by giving a voice to the voiceless, we can make a difference.

Today, in some countries, campaigners for human rights still have reason to fear the knock on the door in the middle of the night. Campaigners and writers and journalists need our support and our prayers. Sometimes we are the ones who are called to speak the truth. If we are to do so with honesty and integrity, we need, first of all, to own the truths about ourselves.

Thought for the day
The truth will set us free.

Prayer
God of all,
I thank you
for all those who bravely speak out the truth.
Help me to own my own truths
and in doing so
to find the freedom that you bring.
Amen.

Fourth Saturday of Lent

Our common humanity

Jr 11:18-20; Ps 7:2-3,9-10,11-12; Jn 7:40-53

'Surely the Messiah does not come from Galilee, does he?'

(John 7:41)

Can any good come out of Galilee? A very similar question is asked of those who come to this country today seeking asylum. Can any good come from Kosovo? Or Afghanistan? Rather than dismissing asylum seekers we need to hear their stories. We have much to learn from them.

In my church, during the past year, we have been listening to the stories of new Londoners and people from ethnic minorities and learning to celebrate the diversity which now makes up British society. A Nigerian woman, living in London, told us her story. She had struggled to bring up her family as a single mother of five in a culture with which she was not familiar. When her passport was stolen she had been put into detention without warning and without trial, accused of being an illegal immigrant. Her children had had to look after themselves. But she was able to regain control of her life, and she now works to support people in detention. Her story caused us all to look again at ourselves and our own sense of identity. Who do we belong to? To London? To England? To Britain? To the church? To humanity?

Today, as we move closer to Holy Week, we suddenly move from externals to focus more on the internal realities: the struggles of Jeremiah between faithfulness to his calling and the reality of his human fears; the struggles of the crowds to understand who Jesus was.

It was hard for the crowds to believe that Jesus was the Messiah. He came from Galilee. Galilee was a place where you found unsophisticated country people. Jesus did not fit in with their preconceptions. They saw him as a jumped-up charlatan.

Sometimes we think of Christ as a type of superman – somehow untouched by the struggle. But Jeremiah and Jesus share a common humanity. Rejection by society had to be borne by Jesus just as Jeremiah had had to bear it.

When we fail to value the humanity of people, we are following the examples of bullies and dictators. We are acting out of power rather than from a sense of our belonging one to another. Just as we need to value the humanity of the weak, so also we must take seriously the humanity of the powerful. The command to love our enemy is a call to recognise the humanity even of those whom we may have to oppose.

Thought for the day

We are a part and parcel of the whole; we cannot find God apart from the rest of humanity

Prayer

God who shared our life in Jesus,
help me to see your face in everyone,
to follow your example
and act for justice out of compassion.
Amen.

Kate McFarlane
Fifth week of Lent

Fifth Sunday of Lent

From fear to faith

Is 43:16-21, Ps 125; Ph 3:8-14; Jn 8:1-11

All I want is to know Christ and the power of his resurrection and to share his sufferings by reproducing the pattern of his death.

(Philippians 3:10)

What was the pattern of Jesus' death? Recurring motifs in the design are his all-embracing love, and his understanding of the needs of those around him. He knew the people who loved him most would yearn desperately for comfort after his death, and so he entrusts them to one another, 'Woman, this is your son. This is your mother.' He is also compassionate towards those who are inflicting the sorrow of his loss upon Mary and John, saying, 'Father forgive them', and in the midst of his own agony he offers hope to the criminal suffering beside him.

Archbishop Oscar Romero of El Salvador proved that it is possible to retrace this pattern. With his passionate concern for the people, with his desire to change the hearts of those who persecuted the poor and killed his friends, and with his determination to continue denouncing injustice despite the threats he received, he faithfully reproduced Jesus' design.

For those of us who are simply grateful not to have been tested in such an extreme situation, so perfect a pattern of compassion and forgiveness seems far beyond our powers. There is, however, another important motif, and that is Jesus' journey through fear to confident trust.

'Why have you forsaken me?' cries Jesus in sorrow, or in anger, to God. On the cross, Jesus penetrated the depths of human pain mentally as well as physically, and he can recognise the helplessness which often confounds and overwhelms us. This vulnerability is part of what it meant for God to become human.

Through the pattern of Jesus' death run the dark strands of doubt as well as the radiant threads of love and trust to which, ultimately, he returns: 'Father, into your hands I commit my spirit.'

There is space then for frailty in our reproduction of the pattern of Jesus' death. There is room for our hesitation. No matter how inadequate we feel for the tasks we face, God is capable of taking and transforming our fears, and of deepening our own imperfect love. We, too, have the potential to move from the hopelessness of, 'Why have you forsaken me?' to the confidence of, 'Into your hands I commit my spirit'.

Thought for the day

During the course of today be aware of areas of your life about which you could turn to God and say, 'Into your hands ...'

Prayer

Loving Jesus,
let the pattern of your death become the pattern of my living.
May each encounter with my own frailty
draw me closer to you.
Lead me forwards from fear to faith.
Amen.

Fifth Monday of Lent

The gift of sight

Dn 13:1-9, 15-17, 19-30, 33-62; Ps 22; Jn 8:1-11

'Let the one among you who is guiltless be the first to throw a stone at her.'

(John 8: 7)

'You're all as bad as each other', might be one way of summing up today's gospel, but that would hardly be good news!

Jesus is confronted here by the human tendency to seek and to exaggerate those things which divide us. The scribes and the Pharisees are so anxious to set themselves apart from the adulterous woman. She is the sinner, the alien, the temptress, the female. Before them, she stands isolated and alone. She is everything from which they wish to distance themselves. They are really accusing her of being 'not like us'. In turning on her they reassert their identity as a group, as the righteous.

Jesus will not let them get away with this. He will not allow them to emphasise what separates them from the woman, but instead gently urges them to see what they share with her. He asks them to look within themselves, knowing that in doing so they will see extraordinary similarities. They will recognise some of the same desires and failings, fears and longings, that they condemn in their victim. They will begin to realise that they share something of her experience, that they have something in common.

This story can be seen as one of Jesus' healing miracles, because the scribes and the Pharisees are having their sight restored. They are being asked to see with the eyes of the sinner, to see the world from her perspective. Jesus is calling them to develop the power of empathy: the ability to enter into the feeling or spirit of someone and appreciate it fully.

Jesus, alone in that crowd, could have claimed to be different and sinless. He alone could have set himself apart, and yet he does not, because he has taken on his humanity fully. He has already chosen to look at the world through the eyes of the human being, and to be compassionate, to suffer with his people. So when we empathise, when we seek to enter into the feelings of another person, we explore the meaning of the incarnation.

Thought for the day

That which unites us as human beings is infinitely greater than that which divides.

Prayer

Jesus Christ,
you embrace our humanity.
Slow my judging
and speed my understanding.
Halt my condemnation
and hasten my compassion.
Grant me the gift of sight.

Amen.

Fifth Tuesday of Lent

The ministry of listening

Nb 21:4-9; Ps 101; Jn 8:21-30

O Lord listen to my prayer
and let my cry for help reach you.

(Psalm 101:1)

I have become very uncomfortable with the idea that in working for justice we should seek to be 'a voice for the voiceless'. How would I feel, I wonder, about someone else taking it upon themselves to know my desires and my needs so entirely that they could express them accurately and truthfully? How would I feel to be told that another person can speak of my life with greater credibility than I could? I would far rather have the power to speak for myself.

I understand, of course, that for many people the opportunities to speak for themselves are scarce. In an unjust and unequal world only some people are considered worth listening to, or are given access to the channels of communication. The poor of our world are remarkably easy to ignore.

In today's psalm a person in need of help cries out to God. The fact that the psalmist is still speaking is itself a sign of hope. Even as he expresses despair, the psalmist still has sufficient confidence to utter his cry, to demand attention, to express his anger at injustice. God has made a commitment to his people and the psalmist is not going to allow God to forget it. If the psalmist truly believed no one was listening he would fall silent.

The role of the listener is thus a vital one, because it gives others a reason to speak. Dietrich Bonhoeffer spoke of listening as being a Christian ministry, a ministry that has been committed to us by God, who is the great listener and in whose work Christians should share.

So rather than claiming to be another person's voice, our task is to listen, and to put ourselves out of our ordinary sphere of action in order to hear the voices of protest. Someone must listen or the voices fall silent. And while we should not impose our interpretation onto another's experience, we have an important role to play in demanding that others listen too. We can turn up the volume of the protest and we can widen the arena in which the sufferers of injustice make their voices heard.

Thought for the day
We will have progressed considerably towards building God's kingdom when all who experience injustice feel it is worthwhile to protest.

Prayer
Faithful God,
your silence is utterly attentive.
May we be humble defenders,
listening advocates,
and truthful witnesses
for the people our world seeks to ignore.
Amen.

Fifth Wednesday of Lent

Good company

Dn 3:14-20, 24-25, 28; Dn 3:52-56; Jn 8:31-42

'We will not serve your god or worship the statue you have erected.'

(Daniel 3: 14)

Like every society, ours has constructed its own new, improved versions of the golden calf in which to put its faith: the nuclear deterrent, consumerism, free trade and market forces. The powerful insist that these are the basis of our freedom, but they have become new forms of slavery, idols in which we have placed our trust.

Our society has also taken pride in destroying what it sees as past idols, and in being sophisticated enough not to need ideologies of any form, from communism to Christianity itself. Individualism has become our creed instead; and when the individual is all-important then there is no need to belong to anything, or to commit ourselves to anything.

Shadrach, Meshach and Abed-Nego, in contrast, show an incredible commitment to their faith, and face the attack on it united. The powers of the state press them to accept its version of the truth, but the three men, speaking with one voice, refuse to worship this false god. Like Jesus himself when he faced his temptations in the wilderness they will not even make use of the situation as an opportunity to test their God. 'If our God, the one we serve, is able to save us from the burning fiery furnace and from your power, he will save us; and even if he does not ... we will not serve your god.'

Theirs is a faith which does not demand signs and proofs. It is faith which when faced with death, is able to say, 'Into your hands I commit my spirit'. It is the faith that holds that it is better to die than to accept the lies of an unjust state.

One of the most difficult aspects of faith is learning how to trust even when there is no sign of God's presence, and when it seems far more logical to agree with the earthly powers that urge us to a comfortable, unquestioning life. It is significant then that at their time of trial Shadrach, Meshach and Abed-Nego face the king together, drawing strength from one another. In that little community of faith lay power far beyond that of a lone individual or of the state itself.

Thought for the day

What are the idols I find myself tempted to serve, and from where do I draw strength to resist them?

Prayer

Challenging God,
discomfort us
when we drift into the worship of the idols of our society,
but comfort us with company
when truth-telling becomes lonely.
Amen.

Fifth Thursday of Lent

Keeping our Covenant

Gn 17:3-9; Ps 104; Jn 8:51-59

'I will make you into nations.'

(Genesis 17: 6)

A year after Hurricane Mitch had spent five days pummelling Honduras I visited communities which were trying to rebuild their homes and their lives. Several communities had adopted similar systems for the construction work: all the houses were being built at the same pace, level by level, everyone being involved in the building of all the houses. Only when the homes were all complete would the ownership of each be decided through a raffle. As a result of the communities' system the same level of skill and effort was going into each property, and everyone gave of their best.

The shared task was drawing the people closer as communities than they had been before the hurricane deprived them of their homes. For some the experience of working together had been so positive that they were planning further projects and considering how to move on to help others outside their immediate community.

We rarely find ourselves in a situation so desperate that we are forced to experience the similarity of our neighbours' needs to our own. It is usually all too easy for us to exist independently of any community, and the word 'community' often remains for us a woolly concept, or, at best, a pleasant ideal.

This is not, however, a living out of the relationship God established with us. From its beginning the Covenant was never purely a relationship between God and the individual. Abraham is only the first of the nations which will emerge from him. It is with a whole people, the people of God, that the Covenant is made: 'You will be my people and I will be your God.'

The Covenant binds us to God, but also to one another, and it is as a community, not merely as individuals, that we maintain it. Our side of the agreement is imperfect and our relationship with God is flawed while people are discriminated against, excluded or ignored. When one of God's people suffers, the others are challenged to right the wrong. Only when justice is established between all the people of God shall we have been true to our Covenant.

Thought for the day
What are the communities of which I feel a part and what do I do which creates or sustains them?

Prayer
God of the promise,
open my heart and my mind
to perceive my need of others and their need of me.
Amen.

Fifth Friday of Lent

Glory to God

Jr 20:10-13; Ps 17; Jn 10:31-42

You say to someone the Father has consecrated and sent into the world, 'You are blaspheming,' because he says, 'I am the Son of God.'

(John 10:36)

'Are they allowed to have these?' called the woman at the checkout, holding aloft an item of underwear. 'They' were asylum seekers trying to use vouchers to pay for their goods in an English supermarket.

One definition of blasphemy is 'contempt or indignity offered to God'. We usually take this to mean taking God's name in vain, making false statements about the nature of God or, as the Jews believed Jesus was doing in today's gospel reading, elevating something unworthy to the state of divinity.

Those confronting Jesus have, of course, misunderstood who Jesus is, but they also have a dangerously limited understanding of blasphemy. God is not so self-absorbed as to be roused only by insults and impostors. We are made in God's image and likeness. We are children of God. Jesus does not only call himself the Son of God, but invites us all to call out: Abba Father. To demean another human being is to show contempt for the creator. Blasphemy lies in treating people unjustly because of their race or religious belief, in policies or practices which are discriminatory, in accumulating wealth at the cost of the livelihoods of others, or in buying goods produced at the expense of people's dignity.

Blasphemy also lies in the degradation of our environment, of which we are called by God to be stewards. It lies in the extermination of species, and in the pollution of our atmosphere, soil and seas. God declared a relationship with the whole of creation. The Covenant was made with 'all living things' not simply with humanity. When we truly embrace our vocation as stewards of creation we give honour to God.

And when we approach each person as a child of God, we are giving glory to the God who made them. In respecting the dignity of each son and daughter of God, we are praising their creator, our Father.

Thought for the day

Are there attitudes I hold towards others which prevent me from seeing them as children of God?

Prayer

Glory be to God.
In our respect for the rights of all human beings,
and in our acceptance of our responsibilities,
in our stewardship of creation,
and in our upholding of the dignity of all God's people,
glory to God in the highest.

Amen.

Fifth Saturday of Lent

The hazardous choice of the Kingdom

Ezk 37:21-28; Jr 31:10-18; Jn 11:45-46

It is better for one man to die for the people, than for the whole nation to be destroyed.

(John 11:50)

It is obvious that those who are benefiting from an unjust regime will do much to maintain the status quo. But an equally strong influence comes from those who are not doing well, but who fear that change would only make things worse.

In today's gospel reading, Caiaphas is determined that the current orthodoxy be maintained. The Israel of Caiaphas was hardly an ideal society for any Jew, since it bore the daily humiliations of being an occcupied territory. Yet Caiaphas would rather maintain an imperfect state where he had some authority, where there was at least some stability, than risk the change heralded by Jesus.

So it is for those of us who live in the wealthy countries of the North. We recognise that the world is not as good as it could be. Global economic changes mean that we are no longer so secure in our jobs; the gap between the rich and the poor is widening; local communities find that it is not always easy to get their voices heard even in a democratic system. Yet perhaps we would rather live with this than risk the radicalism of Christ's kingdom. I cannot help but wonder what might become of me, my lifestyle, my relationships, if I truly followed Christ.

Change, of course, comes anyway, and Caiaphas is powerless to prevent it. So are we. The question for us is whether or not we are going to work wholeheartedly for the kingdom of God. If we choose not to, and settle instead for the status quo, there will still be change – but the changes will be out of our control, dictated by those whose agendas show a complete disregard for justice. If we opt for the kingdom, we embark on a risk-filled journey, where we do not know the final destination and in which we ourselves must be transformed.

When we find the task of building God's kingdom too much for even our most committed efforts, today's gospel reading is profoundly comforting. For even out of Caiaphas' self-seeking agenda God is bringing his own plan to fruition. It is one of the greatest mysteries and encouragements of our faith that God has the power to work even through people and institutions bent on thwarting or side-stepping him.

Thought for the day
The coming of the kingdom of God requires a transformation of the world that can only come when each of us is transformed.

Prayer
Transforming God,
grant me the courage to seek,
wholeheartedly,
the kingdom I claim to desire.
Amen.

Margaret Atkins
Holy week

Passion Sunday

Christ on a cold stone

Lk 19:28-40; Is 50:4-7; Ps 21; Ph 2:6-11; Lk 22:14-23:56

He emptied himself to assume the condition of a slave, and became as all men are.

(Philippians 2:7)

A great work of art helps us to see the familiar in a fresh way. The exhibition at the National Gallery in London, *Seeing Salvation*, concentrated on the ways that Christian art has been used in prayer and devotion, and it focused especially on aspects of the Passion. What can artists help us to see anew in the familiar story of Holy Week?

Today we listen to the grand narrative in St Luke's gospel, from the last supper right through to Jesus' burial. The story rushes on without a break, as Jesus is pushed from pillar to post, interrogated, beaten, insulted, forced to keep on the move, until he is actually nailed to the cross. But suppose that at some point there was a pause. Maybe the cross-beam had not yet arrived from the carpenter's. Suppose Jesus had been left to sit alone and wait, naked except for his crown of thorns. Suppose he had had time to reflect on it all, right in the middle of the story.

In about 1500 an artist from the Netherlands carved a life-size statue of Christ doing just that. He sits on a cold rock, right cheek sunk into his right palm, the elbow pressing heavily onto his knee. The statue was once painted, but today we see bare limestone. Its grey simplicity emphasises the vulnerability of the naked figure. The carving is exquisite, with each detail of the body – finger nails, muscles, bone – perfectly formed and utterly natural. You feel as if he would move if you touched him.

Or perhaps not. For he is profoundly lost in thought. His eyes gaze steadily at the ground ahead. A very slight tension in the muscles around his eyes and lips hints at the depth of his sorrow. We can only guess what he is thinking, but his concentration is total. He knows what he has undertaken and is prepared to continue. In the centre of his grief there is calm. This is what it means to be born in the likeness of men, and he accepts it. He has become obedient unto death, even death on a cross.

Thought for the day
What was Christ thinking in the gaps between the action?

Prayer
Lord,
in the busyness of our lives,
we often feel pushed from pillar to post.
Grant us the space to pause.
Teach us to reflect upon your will with acceptance.
Help us to find calm even in the deepest sorrow.
Amen.

Monday of Holy Week

The true light

Is 42:1-7; Ps 26; Jn 12:1-11

The Lord is my light and my help: whom shall I fear?

(Psalm 26:1)

The New Testament writers almost never describe Jesus directly as God. Instead, they ascribe to him roles or titles reserved in the Hebrew Scriptures for God alone: judge, saviour, Lord, and so on. When St John called Jesus the 'true light' he was picking up Old Testament language in this way: 'my light and my help'. At the same time, he echoes Isaiah: 'a light to the nations'.

The theme of Christ as the light of the world is tailor-made for artists. Take, for example, the painting of the nativity at night by a fifteenth-century artist called Geertgen tot Sint Jans. The tiny, delicate baby lies surrounded by his mother and some child-like angels. Most of the painting is in sombre browns and blacks. Only the child glows, white and gold in his crib; fine golden rays of light stream from him. The faces bent over him shine too, with the light that reflects from him, innocent in their wonder. In the gloom behind, you can dimly discern the outline of a large and curious cow, a mild-faced donkey, and a nervous, over-awed Joseph. Deep in the background is the angel appearing to the shepherds; the gleam of the angel's wings and the shepherds' fire are feeble compared with the light from the newborn baby.

In front of the crib there is a dark space, which seems very near. It seems to draw the viewer into the picture. We too are invited to come in from the dark, and bend over the Christ. We are to see his light and to reflect it ourselves.

Without light we can neither see nor be seen. St John's claim is striking in its implications. Unless we see the world in the way revealed by this man, we are stumbling in the shadows. Only through his proclamation of the kingdom, through his welcoming of the outcast, through his clear-eyed embrace of suffering, through his radical trust in the Father, do we see the world as it really is. And only by looking at him will we become visible, when his light is reflected in our faces.

Thought for the day
The light of Christ reveals the world as it really is.

Prayer
Lord,
help us to see the world clearly
in the light of Christ.
Help us to reflect his light in our own faces.
Illuminate for us the dark corners which we prefer to ignore.
Amen.

Tuesday of Holy Week

The traitors

Is 49:1-6; Ps 70; Jn 13:21-33, 36-38

Peter said to him, 'Why can't I follow you now? I will lay down my life for you.'

(John 13:37)

The images I have chosen today originally formed two of the four sides of a small ivory casket. It dates from the fifth century, and depicts the story of the crucifixion and resurrection. The figures on it are squat, lively and strong, and the small spaces crowded with action. In the first one, Pilate sits at the left, washing his hands. Jesus strides powerfully through the middle, carrying his cross, about to pass Peter. Peter is sitting beneath the cockerel, his arm outstretched in a profession of innocence, as if to say, 'Would I betray you?' Or perhaps he is not talking to Jesus, but to the man behind, who points at him accusingly. Perhaps he is saying, 'Me – could I be a Galilean?' The same gesture would do for both.

In the second scene, a tree on the left is balanced by the cross on the right. From the tree hangs Judas, physically and mentally broken. Silver coins spill uselessly from the bag on the ground beneath his dead feet. Christ is dying too on the cross, but he looks strong and majestic. This is not a late medieval lament, but a robust Roman representation of confidence in the Son of God. Even Mary and John seem calm beneath the cross, and

Longinus, the soldier who recognised Christ when he pierced him with a lance, looks up at him in wonder.

The three betrayed Christ each in his own way: Pilate, because he lacked a true passion for justice, Peter because he lacked courage. Both made empty gestures, and both, this carving suggests, came to look utter fools.

But what of Judas? Here, perhaps there is a surprise. The tree on which he hangs is leafy. It even has a small bird in its branches. Could this also be the tree of life? Judas does not look silly, but pitiful. He hangs there, completely passive. Our eyes are drawn from him to the other tree. Here the wood is dead, but Jesus' dying body appears full of strength. Is there power enough here to bring life and forgiveness even to Judas? Perhaps so. Why else place the two trees side by side?

Thought for the day

Is it right to divide the world into Peters and Judases, or does the cross of Christ reach beyond the divide?

Prayer

Lord,
we betray you through apathy,
through cowardice,
through greed.
Turn our apathy into passion,
our cowardice into courage,
our greed into generosity.
Forgive us our sins,
and help us to pray for forgiveness for others.

Amen.

Wednesday of Holy Week

The man of sorrows

Is 50:4-9; Ps 68; Mt 26:14-25

For my part I made no resistance,
neither did I turn away.

(Isaiah 50: 5)

The Holy Week liturgy exploits the whole repertoire of Old Testament expressions of grief: Isaiah's servant-songs, the psalms of lament, the book of Lamentations itself. It is time to contemplate Christ the man of sorrows. Here is another picture from the fifteenth-century Netherlands. It is a full-face image of Christ, wearing the crown of thorns and a white robe, his hands crossed in front of him, holding up the mock sceptre the soldiers gave him and the birch with which they flogged him.

The picture both develops, and subverts, traditional imagery. The pose is that of a royal portrait, complete with crown, robes and instruments of office. This is doubly ironic. The king is, of course, a helpless victim; even his wrists are bound together in front of him. Yet at a deeper level, he is, truly, king; and his power lies in his very weakness.

The face is very similar to the traditional Eastern icon of Christ. The forked beard, central parting, long nose, rounded eyebrows: all these are familiar. But his eyes are bloodshot, and large tears roll down his cheeks, glistening in the light. The calm, majestic Christ can also weep.

The eyes are startling. Their redness and their tears are utterly life-like. But they retain the icon's traditional gaze: one eye looks directly at the viewer; the other focuses at a slight angle into the distance. Is he weeping for his own suffering? He does not seem to be. When we weep for our own pain, we turn inward, closing our eyes, hunching our shoulders and shutting out the world. But the thoughts of this man move outwards. This is not just sorrow, but compassion.

'I did not cover my face against insult and spittle' (Isaiah 50:6). Jesus was not reduced to terror or self-pity by his enemies. He looked them in the face. But what was he thinking when he caught Judas' eye at the meal, or watched Pilate during his trial? What was in his mind as his eyes swept the hostile crowd, or rested on the bullying soldiers? When he wept, how much of his grief was for them?

Thought for the day

When Jesus wept, who was he weeping for?

Prayer

Lord,
grant us the strength,
even in our own times of sorrow,
to look outward with compassion
upon the needs of others.
Amen.

Maundy Thursday

The bound lamb

Ex 12:1-8, 11-14; Ps 115; I Co 11:23-26; Jn 13:1-15

'It must be an animal without blemish, a male one year old; you may take it from either sheep or goats.'

(Exodus 12: 5)

We usually forget the lamb's point of view. We hear in Exodus how the lamb is chosen carefully, and then kept for fourteen days. Next it is slaughtered. Its blood is daubed on the door-posts, and it is roasted and hastily consumed. Some of us have eaten lamb together to celebrate a *seder* meal on Maundy Thursday. We think about the lamb as a mere object, always from our point of view: is it suitable for sacrifice? Is it tasty? But what is it like for the lamb?

The Spanish painter Francisco de Zurbarán asked himself that. He became fascinated by painting lambs. In his picture 'The Bound Lamb' the lamb is lying, neck outstretched, on a grey slab. The background is completely black, so that the lamb stands out starkly. Its slim, stiff legs are bound together, wrists and ankles, as it were, crossed and held by thin brown rope. The lamb is captured with photographic precision: the eyelashes, the curved horns, the curling wool, are all so natural you seem to feel their texture.

A strong young body, full of vigour. It ought to be skipping in a field. Here, it is utterly helpless. It is twisted unnaturally by the rope, but calm. There is no effort to struggle. It simply tries to find a way of resting in this strange, uncomfortable position. Is it still afraid? Does it know what will happen next?

The sub-title of Zurbarán's picture is *Agnus Dei*, 'Lamb of God'. Aha, we say. It is supposed to be a metaphor for Christ. We are used to that. Christ is like the lamb led to the slaughter. It sounds comfortable, and familiar. But the genius of Zurbarán's picture is that it is not metaphorical. This lamb is stunningly realistic. This is what it is actually like to be a lamb tied for the slaughter. There is nothing symbolic about this rope. It reminds us that the title 'Lamb of God' does not separate Christ from the rest of humanity. Whenever people's hands and feet are tied, by slavery or imprisonment, by poverty or debt, by grief or depression, by sickness or death, then the lamb shares their lot.

Thought for the day

When we think of others as objects, it is easy to leave them in chains.

Prayer

Lord,
help us to remember all those enslaved by the systems of which we are a part.
Help us to see things from their point of view.
Help us to ask if we can untie their ropes.
Help us to recall how a lamb moves when it is free.

Amen.

Good Friday

Handling the body

Is 52:13-53.12; Ps 30; Heb 4:14-16, 5:7-9; Jn 18:1-19.42

They took the body of Jesus.

(John 19:40)

Have you ever wondered how heavy Jesus was? Ugolino di Nerio had to think about it. For he painted the scene of Christ's body being removed from the cross for the altarpiece of Santa Croce in Florence.

A grey-headed Joseph of Arimathea is half-way up a ladder which leans against the centre of the cross-beam. His left arm is hooked around the beam, his right supporting Jesus' chest. St John stands on the right, holding the waist from behind. The Virgin receives the head and shoulders, as if in a lifeless embrace. At the foot of the cross Nicodemus kneels to remove the nail from his feet with a pair of black iron pliers.

They are doing a difficult job. Joseph grimaces with the effort of keeping his balance. John and Mary are bent, with the weight as much as with grief. Nicodemus frowns as he tugs at the nail. The problem is not just to get the body down, but to do so with gentleness. The careful tenderness of their actions is captured to perfection.

On Good Friday we focus on the suffering of Jesus before and during his execution. But for a third of the day he does not suffer at all. He is simply dead. How do we reflect on this? Artists show us the dead body, and invite a tender response. But we cannot comfort a dead body. This body hurt when it was flogged and nailed. But now it can feel neither pain nor consolation. Why treat it with such compassion?

Joseph and Nicodemus, Mary and John, did not know the end of the story. They could not give their grief a short-cut. From now on, they believed, the world was a world without this man whom they had loved. His body was now a sign of his absence, not his presence. They could no longer honour him: he was not there. But at least they could honour his memory. Perhaps we too should pause a moment with them, and ponder the memory of the dead man. It is all too easy to let our minds race ahead to the resurrection.

Thought for the day
Jesus' friends did not know that he would rise again.

Prayer
Lord,
bring comfort to the bereaved,
bring faith to those who have no hope of resurrection,
bring joy to those who fear that Christ is absent from the world.
Amen.

Holy Saturday

Between heaven and earth

Gn 1:1-2.2; Rm 6:3-11; Ps 117; Lk 24:1-12

*In the beginning God created the heavens
and the earth.*

(Genesis 1:1)

The most striking of all the images in the exhibition *Seeing Salvation* was Salvador Dalí's 'Christ of St John of the Cross'. The canvas is huge. Christ hangs on a cross, high above the world. The cross is slanted towards us, and we see it from above. Jesus' neck is bent, so that we see the top of his head and shoulders. The beautiful young body is caught in light, and casts a sharp shadow on the cross-beam. This is a God's-eye view. We look down upon the crucifixion, just as the Father might have looked down. Perhaps the light that falls on Jesus is the radiance of the Father.

Behind is blackness. But far below is the earth. There is a cloudy sky, a hint of sunrise over the tiny mountains in the distance, a lake with a boat. There are two fishermen, going about their ordinary business. It is a specific place, Port Lligat in Spain, where Dalí lived and worked. The cross bridges the gap between the Father and everyday life.

A crucifixion: the obvious day to reflect on this is Good Friday. But this is an image which takes us beyond Christ's death. Or rather, it is an image which takes

Christ's death and stretches it across the universe. Above every tiny fishing-port, above every country village, above every busy city, above farmland and forest and mountains, hovers the cross of Christ.

'In the beginning God created the heavens and the earth.' The Easter Vigil tells the story from the start. It is a story of a specific people, Israel, and of a specific person, Jesus. But the context is the story of the whole world. Every human and animal life, however humble or insignificant, is caught up in this.

The stories of creation and of redemption are one and the same. The young man who died on the cross is the one through whom all things were made. The radiant light which falls across his shoulders hints at the resurrection. The resurrection, it seems, is hovering over the earth, reaching down from God to every fisherman below.

Thought for the day

The cross of Christ reaches down from the Father to every living creature.

Prayer

Lord,
teach us gratitude for the world you have made,
teach us respect for every living creature,
teach us to see one another in the light of the
resurrection.
Amen.

Easter Sunday

The resurrection in Cookham

Ac 10:34, 37-43; Ps 117; Col 3:1-4; Jn 20:1-9

But when Christ is revealed – and he is your life – you too will be revealed in all your glory with him.

(Colossians 3:4)

Place: Cookham churchyard, Berkshire.
Time: the Second Coming.

Well, what do you think it will be like? The artist Stanley Spencer imagined the general resurrection taking place in his home village. His picture is gloriously full of activity. Grave-slabs are opening everywhere, as the inhabitants of Cookham climb back into new life. Some are wearing long white night-robes, others their ordinary clothes, others are naked. They are stretching, yawning, greeting one another. One lady smells a flower; another brushes down her husband's jacket, as if it was the most natural thing in the world. In the background we can glimpse the river, where a pleasure-boat is carrying people to heaven. In the middle is Christ himself, enthroned in the church porch, which is covered with rose-blossom. He is dressed in white, and his arms are full of babies, which he gently rocks, a merciful judge. The artist himself dozes contentedly in the sun on top of a gravestone in the foreground. A place he knows. People he knows. Here is the resurrection of the just.

How are we to imagine the future resurrection? The New Testament gives us accounts of the risen Jesus: we can make some guesses from that. It also provides images: the heavenly banquet, the new Jerusalem. There is only a little to go on. There are two dangers here. We might think we know exactly what heaven is like by imagining it too literally. But more likely we will do the opposite: be so afraid of getting it wrong that we don't think about it at all.

We need the artists. They take the risks for us. They liberate our imaginations. We might rejoice in the simple pleasures of Spencer's painting. We might find it all just too cosy. But whichever, he challenges us to share his adventure. Do we really connect the resurrection with our everyday lives? Easter is about the ordinary people we know, in Cookham or in Calcutta, in Birmingham or in Belgrade.

The promise of resurrection is for them – for us. Do we dare to imagine that?

Thought for the day

What will it be like to 'appear with him in glory'?

Prayer

Lord,
help us to bring the joy of Easter
to those with whom we live.
May the resurrection of Christ transform our lives,
in this age and in the age to come.

Amen.